THE ALLISON CONTEMPORARY PIANO COLLECTION

Repertoire suitable for Auditions in the National Guild of Piano Teachers

Compiled and classified by
Julia Amada Kruger, Vice President of the American College of
Musicians/National Guild of Piano Teachers

Copyright 1993
by
Keyboard Creations

Printed in the U.S.A. by
Davis Brothers, Waco, TX 76711

FOREWORD

We are pleased to provide teachers with a new and exciting format for piano literature expressly designed for Auditions in the National Guild of Piano Teachers. This series is a classified compilation of Guild members' works with appropriate Musicianship Phases and IMMT. We hope you will find this series extremely useful and a valuable addition to the Guild library.

I would like to offer my appreciation and thanks to those who donated their works to the project as well as those persons involved in its completion.

Richard Allison
President,
American College of Musicians,
National Guild of Piano Teachers

ACKNOWLEDGEMENT

Special acknowledgement and appreciation to Darryl Dunn of KeyNote Productions; and to Joseph M. Martin; Austin, Texas

Photograph used by permission of the Yamaha Corporation

Use of this photograph does not constitute an endorsement of the product by either the American College of Musicians/ National Guild of Piano Teachers or the publisher.

TABLE OF CONTENTS

EE CLASSIFICATION

Joyce Schatz Pease	*Jessica's Waltz*	1
Lois Rehder Holmes	*Seascape*	3
Joseph M. Martin	*Blue Elephant*	5
John Robert Poe	*Sir Abelard's Lament*	7
David Karp	*El Torero*	9
Mary Ann Parker	*Tall Tale*	12
LeAnn Halvorson	*Turn About*	13
Blythe Owen	*Dance of the Honeybees*	15
Carol Klose	*Transylvania Ball*	17
Martin Cuellar	*Making a Wish*	20
Vera Wills	*Voyage to the Moon*	21
David Angerman	*Woodchuck Chase*	23
James Michael Stevens	*Winter Solace*	25

EF CLASSIFICATION

Karen Munson	*Three Canons*	26
Rev. Kevin E. Cray	*Hoedown*	28
Martin Cuellar	*Toccatina*	30
Patricia W. King	*Frantic!*	32
Carol Klose	*Meditation*	35
Lois Rehder Holmes	*Rhythmic Dance*	36
David Karp	*Dance Allegro*	38

MUSICIANSHIP PHASES

Level EE	40
Level EF	45

Jessica's Waltz

Joyce Schatz Pease

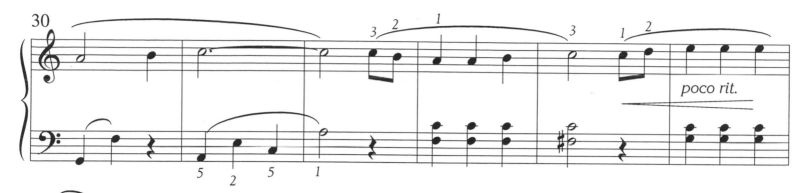

C Major (hands separately or together)

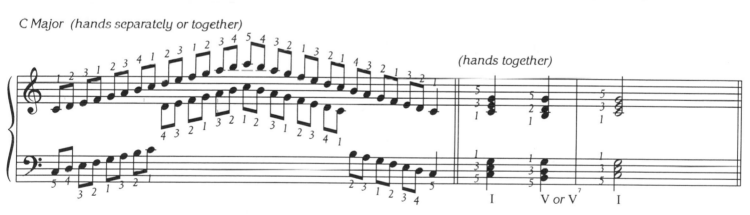

Seascape

for Jerald Thomas Sames

Lois Rehder Holmes

D harmonic minor (hands separately or together)

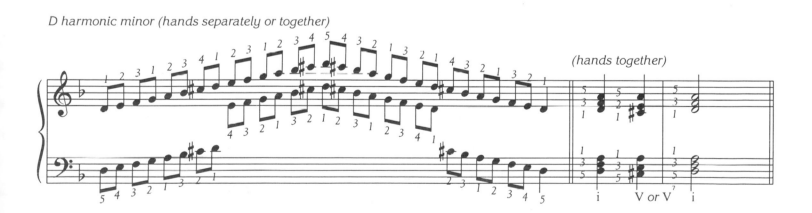

Blue Elephant

Joseph M. Martin

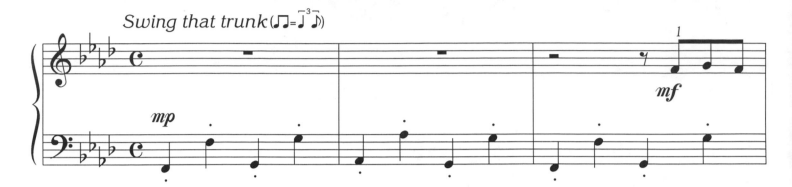

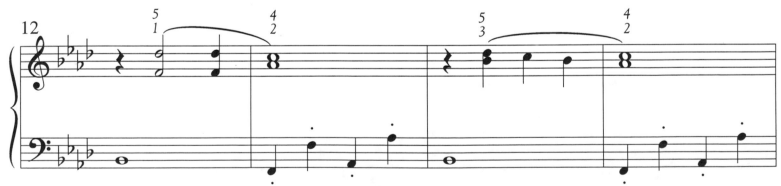

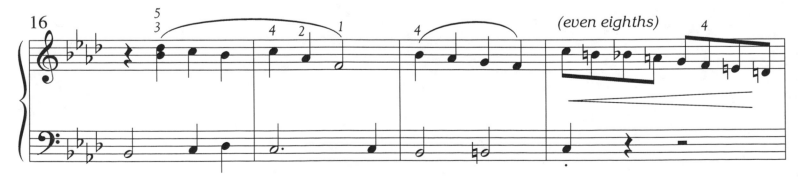

F harmonic minor (hands separately or together)   *(hands together)*

Sir Abelard's Lament

John Robert Poe

El Torero

for Dr. Willard Palmer

David Karp

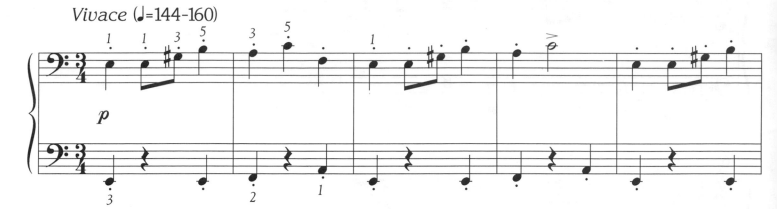

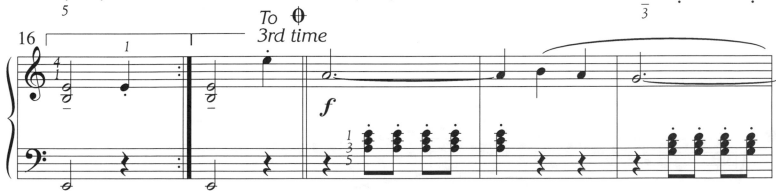

D.C. al Coda

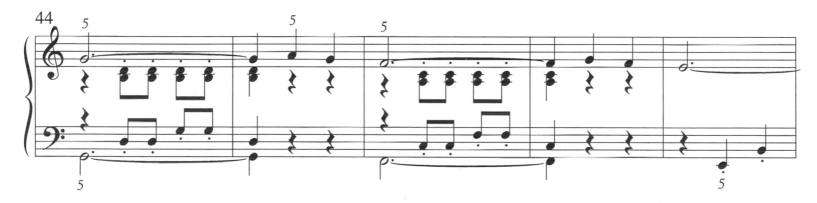

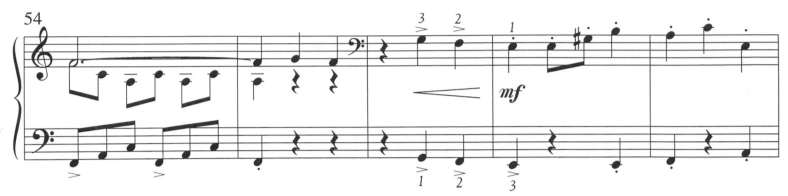

A harmonic minor (hands separately or together)

(hands together)

i   V or V⁷   i

Tall Tale

Mary Ann Parker

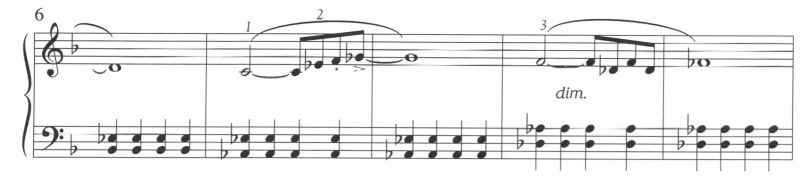

12

Turn About

LeAnn Halvorson

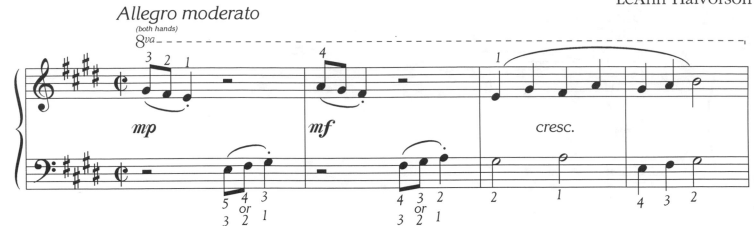

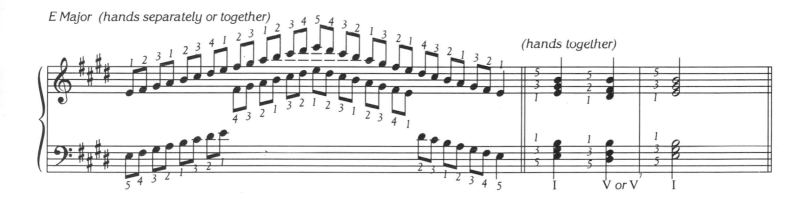

Dance Of The Honeybees

Blythe Owen

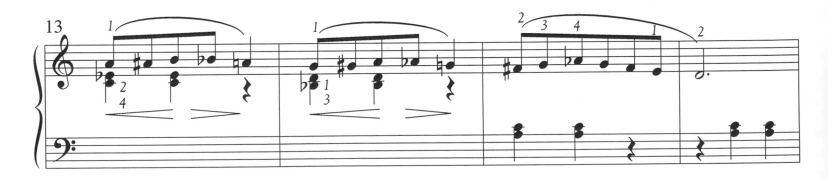

(Chromatic: No IMMT Required)

Transylvania Ball

Carol Klose

Eerily bright waltz tempo (♩=168)

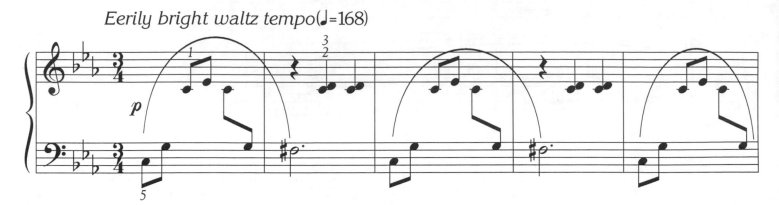

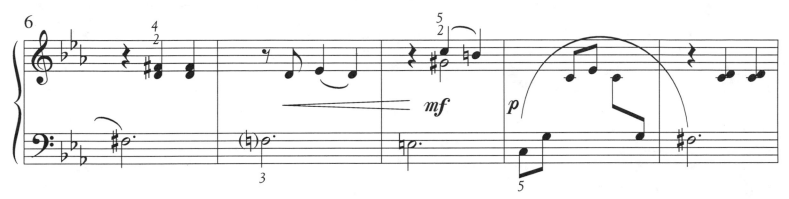

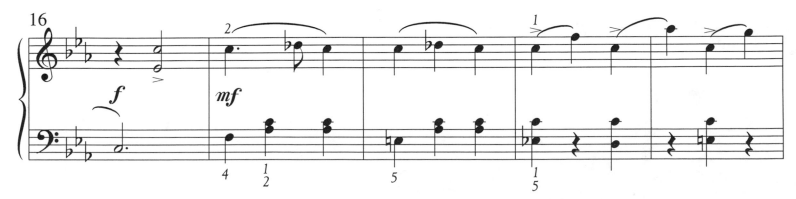

The sun's first rays

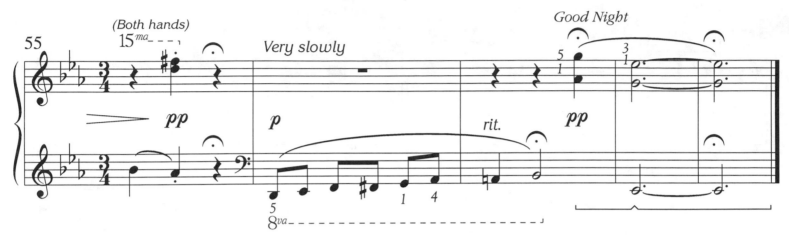

Good Night

Very slowly

C harmonic minor (hands separately or together)

(hands together)

i   V or V⁷   i

Making A Wish

from "Birthday Suite"

Martin Cuellar

Allegro, ma non tanto

(stems up - R.H.; stems down - L.H.)

una corda throughout

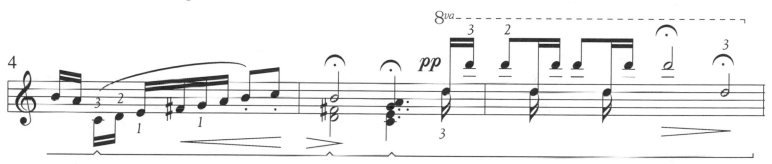

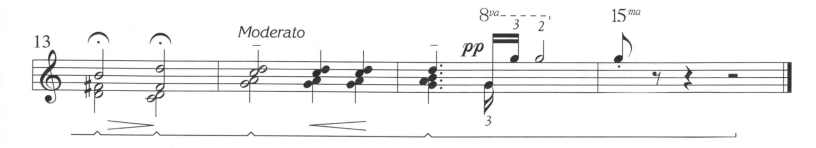

(Modal: No IMMT Required)

Voyage To The Moon

Vera Wills

21

A harmonic minor (hands separately or together)

(hands together)

i   V or V[7]   i

Woodchuck Chase

David Angerman

F Major (hands separately or together)

(hands together)

Winter Solace

James Michael Stevens

G harmonic minor (hands separately or together)

Three Canons

I

Karen Munson

II

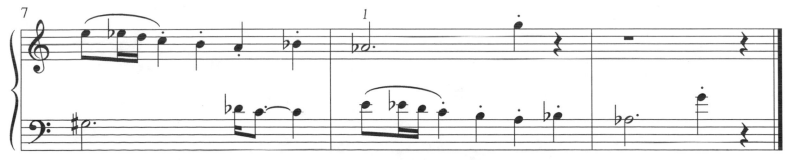

26

III

Fearfully

(Polytonal: No IMMT Required)

Hoedown

Kevin E. Cray

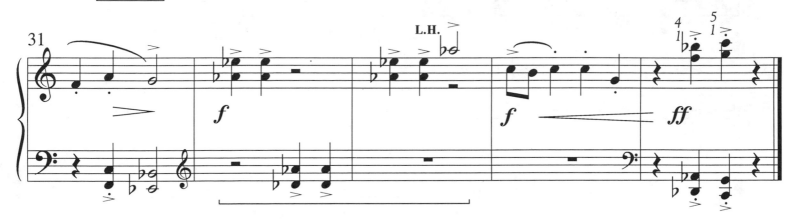

C Major *(hands separately or together)*

I   V or V⁷   I

Toccatina

Martin Cuellar

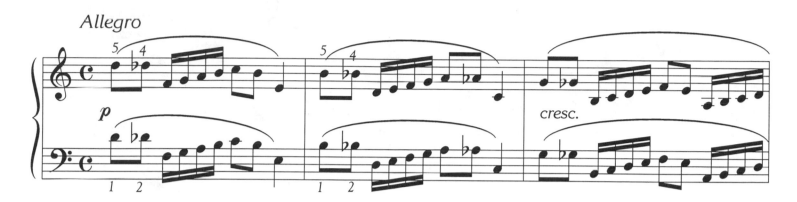

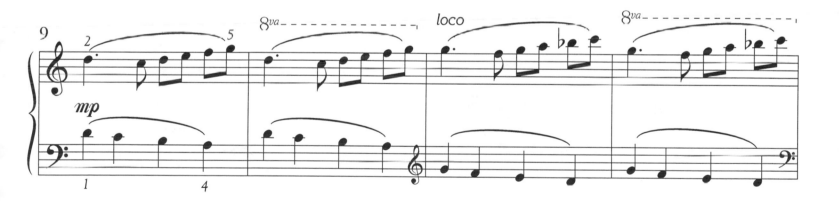

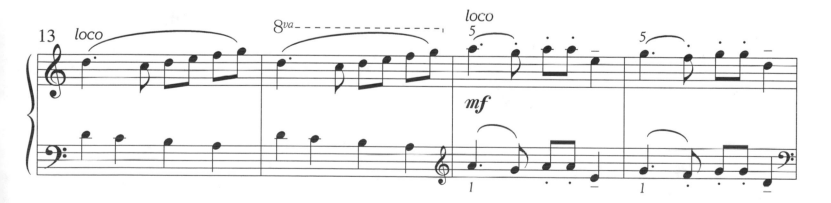

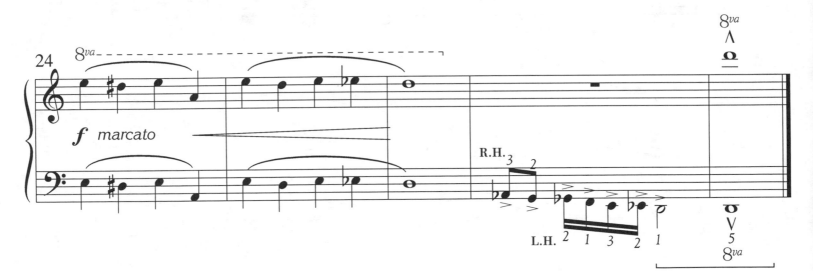

(Modal: No IMMT Required)

Frantic!

Patricia W. King

As fast as possible

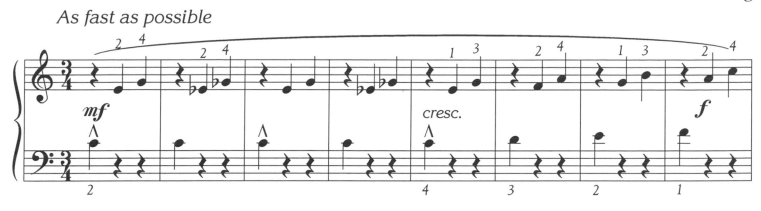

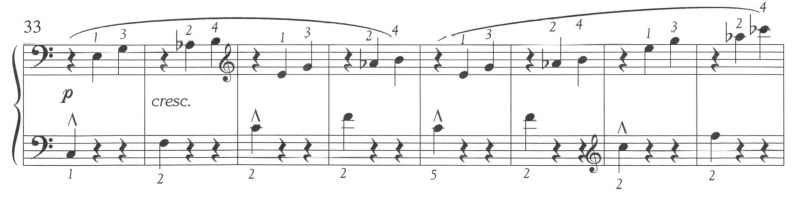

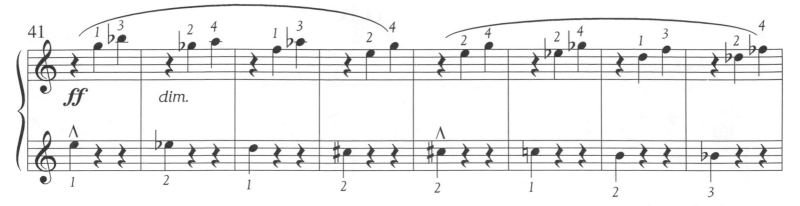
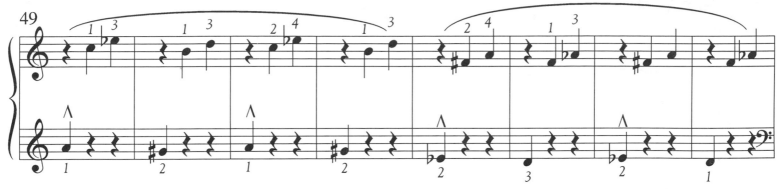
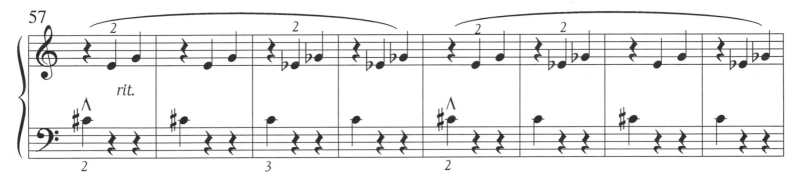
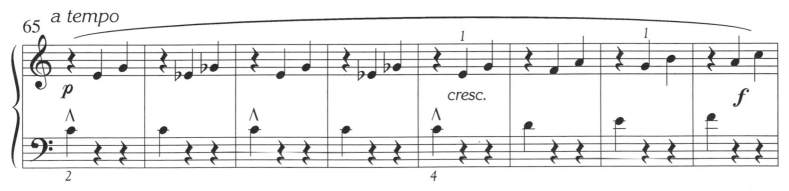
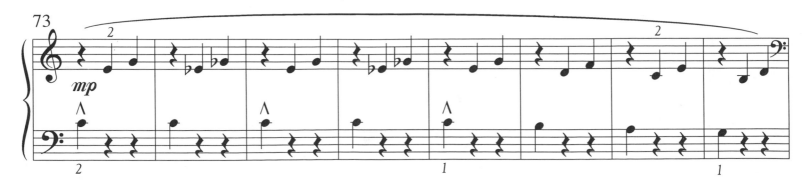

C Major *(hands separately or together)*

(hands together)

I   V or V⁷   I

Meditation

Carol Klose

Slowly and thoughtfully, with much expression

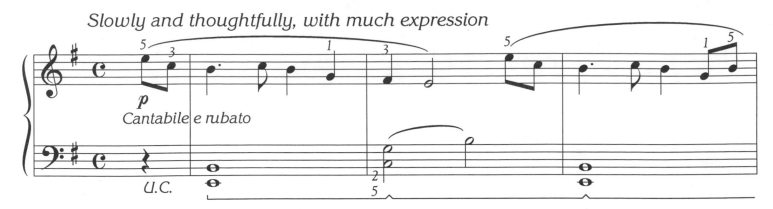

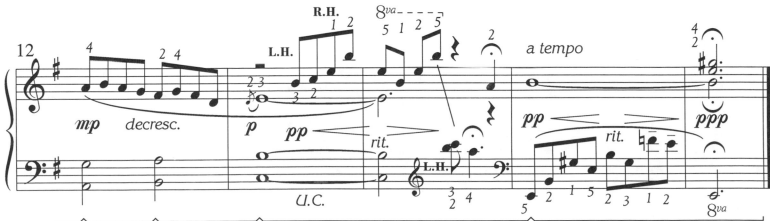

Rhythmic Dance

for Giovannina Elena Morelli

Lois Rehder Holmes

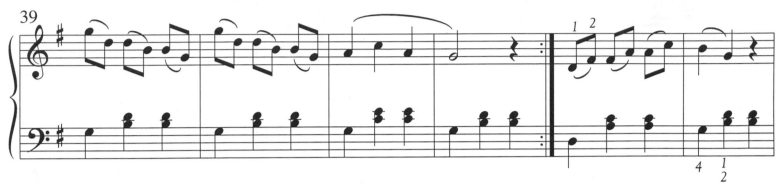

G harmonic minor (hands separately or together)

i   V or V⁷   i

Dance Allegro

for Margaret Pilar Rejino

David Karp

Allegro (♩=c. 168)

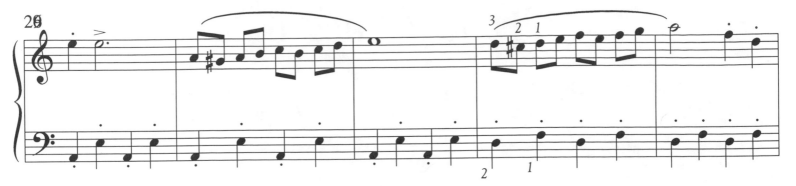

G harmonic minor (hands separately or together)

(hands together)

i   V or V⁷   i

MUSICIANSHIP PHASES
EE Classification
(Fingerings are suggestions, not requirements)

Scales: (separately or together)

(Majors)

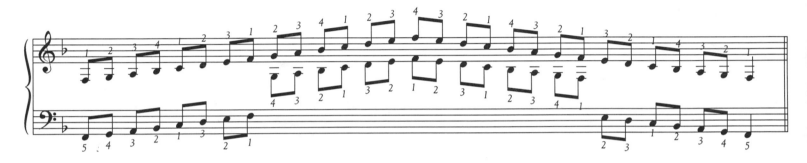

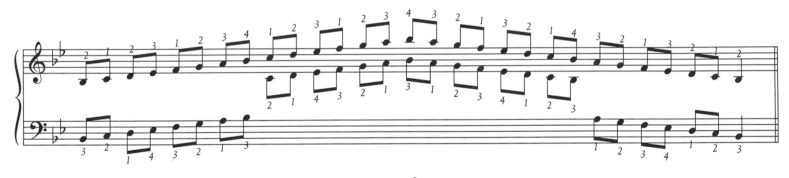

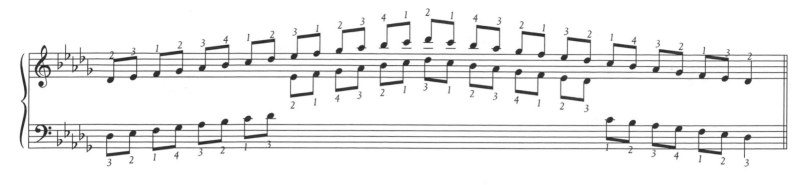

Chords: (hands separately)
(Majors)

Cadences: (hands together)
(Majors)

I   V₇   I
or V

Arpeggios: (separately or together)
(see Syllabus for metronomic requirement)

(Majors)

See Guild Syllabus for additional Phases:
Ear Training, Transposition,
Improvisation, and Sight-Reading.

EF Classification
(Fingerings are suggestions, not requirements)

Scales: (separately or together)
(harmonic minors)

Musicianship Phases
© Copyright 1993 ACM/NGPT

Chords: (separately or together)
(minors)

Cadences: (hands together)

(minors)

i V₇ i
or V

Arpeggios: (separately or together)

(see Syllabus for metronomic requirements)

(minors)

See Guild Syllabus for additional Phases:
Ear Training, Transposition,
Improvisation, and Sight-Reading.

TEACHER'S NOTES:

TEACHER'S NOTES:

TEACHER'S NOTES: